ANIMAL GROSSAPEDIA

MELISSA STEWART

SCHOLASTIC INC.

10 9 8 7 6 5 4 3 2 1   12 13 14 15 16

Printed in the U.S.A.   40
First edition, September 2012

Book design by Kay Petronio

CONTENTS

GROSS
OR
GREAT?

SNOT. POOP. PEE. We humans think these gross, gooey, stinky substances are totally disgusting!

But here's a surprise: Some animals have a very different view of this yucky stuff. Burrowing owls collect poop. Desert tortoises use pee for protection. And camels puke on one another when they're mad! Yep, it's true. Want to know more? Well, **UR-INE** luck!

DUNG BEETLES

Dung beetles shape the poop for their eggs into balls that weigh up to fifty times more than they do

What do scientists call the little black bugs that spend all their time in, on, or near poop? The name shouldn't surprise you: "DUNG beetles."

No doubt about it—dung beetles have a fondness for poop. They live in it. They eat it. (To them, it's delicious *and* nutritious.) And guess where they lay their eggs. That's right. Female dung beetles lay their eggs inside giant balls of poop. When the beetle grubs hatch, they're surrounded by food.

When a koala is born, it's the size of a jelly bean. The mini **MARSUPIAL**, or joey, climbs into its mom's pouch and stays put for more than six months.

At first, the little joey feeds on nothing but mother's milk. But eventually, it begins to eat pap—soft, runny poop full of **BACTERIA** from its mother.

Koalas eat poisonous eucalyptus leaves, but don't get sick, because the bacteria in their bodies break down the poison. Thanks to those bacterial buddies from mother's pap, adult koalas can munch on eucalyptus all day long.

KOALAS

A joey stays with its mom for about a year. During that time, she teaches her youngster how to choose just the right eucalyptus leaves.

AFRICAN BUSH ELEPHANTS

By the time an elephant becomes an adult, it may eat three hundred pounds of plants each day.

oeys aren't the only baby MAMMALS that dine on poop. In fact, lots of young animals eat it—even elephant calves.

Just fifteen minutes after an elephant is born, it stands up and starts gulping milk from its mom. The little one can drink up to three gallons a day.

After six months, the calf's diet changes. It starts eating leaves and grass—and the poop of its family and friends. Its body needs the bacteria in adult elephant poop to DIGEST the tough plants that grow on the African plains.

A female panda gives birth inside a cave or hollow tree. And she stays there with her little one for up to four months. During that time, she laps up her baby's poop. It's the best way to keep her cub safe. That way, hungry leopards won't be able to sniff out the helpless cub.

GIANT PANDAS

A newborn panda is completely helpless. Its eyes are shut, and it has no teeth or fur. When the cub is about eight months old, it begins to eat bamboo on its own. But the youngster stays with its mom for up to three years.

COTTONTAIL RABBITS

By digesting grass twice, a rabbit gets an extra supply of the vitamins and sugars it needs to live and grow.

Rabbits may look cute and cuddly, but they have a pretty disgusting habit. They devour their droppings daily.

A rabbit eats grass, and grass is hard to digest. So once a day, a rabbit produces CECOTROPES— soft, shiny pellets full of partially digested food.

A rabbit can't resist eating the pellets.

As cecotropes travel through the rabbit's gut, bacteria get a second chance to break down the grass and absorb important NUTRIENTS. Finally, the rabbit produces a second batch of droppings, which it doesn't eat.

Burrowing Owls don't eat poop, they collect it. Lots of it. And they aren't picky about the source. They like horse poop, cow poop, dog poop, even pig poop.

So what do the little birds do with their prize collections? They use it to line their underground nests. A poop-lined nest attracts insects in search of food. And that means the owls can have a feast of their own. In fact, owls with **DUNG** in their **DWELLINGS** attract ten times more dung beetles than owls with better-smelling burrows.

BURROWING OWLS

Most owls are nocturnal, or active at night, but burrowers come out during the day. They live in large groups and raise their owlets underground.

LEAFCUTTER ANTS

An ant colony is like a family. It's made up of a queen and all her children. As many as eight million leafcutter ants can live together in a single colony.

Every day, thousands of leafcutter ants march into the rain forest. They climb up trees and cut leaves into tiny pieces. Then they carry the pieces back to their nest.

But the hardworking ants don't eat the leaves. They'd rather nibble on fields of **FUNGI** growing inside their nest.

So why do the ants need the leaves? They chew the leaves into a mushy green paste and spit it onto their fungus gardens. The leafy mush helps the fungi grow.

But the tiny farmers don't stop there. They also **FERTILIZE** their food supply with their own poop.

WOLVERINES

A wolverine isn't much bigger than a house cat, but it's one of the toughest animals on Earth. Thanks to its razor-sharp claws and bone-crushing jaws, a wolverine can fight off wolves, cougars, and even grizzly bears.

In winter, a wolverine dines on dead elk, deer, and caribou. After it feeds, it sprays its old meal with foul-smelling fluid from its behind, spoiling it for other hungry hunters.

Wolverines live in the far North, where the nights are long, the days are cold, and the snow is deep.

Fieldfares live in forests and scrublands in Europe and Asia. They often nest in small colonies.

At mating time, a female fieldfare builds a neat nest near the top of a tree. After laying her eggs, she works hard to protect her home. If an enemy gets too close, bombs away! The devoted mama poops on the predator.

After the chicks are born, their dad gets in on the action. He and his mate take turns feeding the little ones and showering poop on enemies.

FIELDFARES

HIPPOPOTAMUSES

Most of the time hippos are gentle giants, but never get between a hippo and the water. A hippo can outrun you on land and outswim you in the water. You don't stand a chance against an angry hippo!

ome people say hippopotamuses are real stinkers. This reputation is, at least in part, due to the fact that they fling their poop.

During the day, a hippo lounges lazily in a water hole. Each night, it moves to land and eats about 150 pounds of grass. Lots of food equals lots of poop.

Just before a hippo relieves itself, it starts spinning its tail. So as poop exits, it sprays in every direction.

Why does a hippo shoot its poop far and wide? Nobody knows for sure. Maybe it sends a message to other hippos: "Here I am!" Or it might help the hippo find its way back to its water hole. After all, hippos can't see very well.

All pooped out? Okay, then let's talk about pee. The Siberian chipmunk lives in the forests of northern Asia. And it has lots of enemies. Snakes. Hawks. Weasels. Foxes. They all think the chipmunk is deee-licious.

That would be bad news for some little critters. But the clever chipmunk knows how to stay safe.

When it spots a dead snake, it bites into its enemy's **BLADDER**. After the urine drains out, the chipmunk takes a bath in the pee.

It might sound gross, but it's actually pretty smart. The snake's strong scent keeps predators away.

SIBERIAN CHIPMUNKS

Siberian chipmunks spend most of their time searching for seeds, nuts, mushrooms, berries, and insects on the ground. At night, they sleep inside deep burrows.

ven though a desert tortoise has built-in body armor, it's no match for coyotes, cougars, or golden eagles. So when one of these enemies gets too close, a tortoise freezes to blend in with its rocky surroundings.

If that doesn't work, the tortoise has one final trick. When a hunter grabs a tortoise, the resourceful reptile empties its bladder. A mouthful of pee would make any predator lose its appetite.

Desert Tortoises also use urine to protect their young. After a female tortoise buries her eggs, she pees all over the ground. The stinky urine prevents hungry foxes and lizards from smelling the eggs. And it keeps the eggs moist.

DESERT TORTOISES

Each year, a female desert tortoise produces between four and twelve eggs. Each one is the size of a Ping-Pong ball. After about three months, the eggs hatch and the tiny tortoises dig to the surface.

GOATS

People started raising goats for their meat and milk about nine thousand years ago. Today, about two hundred kinds of goats live in the United States.

When a boy is trying to get a girl's attention, he might give her flowers or candy. But that's not what a male goat does. Not by a long shot.

Instead, the buck rubs his face and beard in his own pee. He spreads some on his front legs, too. Then he walks up to the female that interests him most.

And guess what—she likes it. In fact, she urinates, too. The buck puts his nose in the female's pee and sniffs. If he likes what he smells, he curls his upper lip and the goats become a couple.

Goats aren't the only animals that use urine to attract mates. Squirrels, rabbits, foxes, and porcupines use it, too. So do crabs and lobsters. But male lobsters also use urine in a whole different way.

Most animals have one bladder, but a lobster has two. They're on either side of the clawed critter's head.

When two males meet, they wage war by blasting each other with pee. They can shoot their stinky streams more than six feet!

Chemicals in lobster urine relay information about the owner's size and strength. So if the smaller lobster is smart, he backs away.

AMERICAN LOBSTERS

Bladders in the head? That's not the only strange thing about a lobster's body. Its brain is in its throat, and its teeth are in its stomach. It listens with its legs and tastes with its feet.

TURKEY VULTURES

A turkey vulture's bald red head might look ugly, but it comes in handy. When the bird chows down on a dead animal, it sticks its whole head inside the carcass to reach the meat. Bits of rotten flesh would cling to a feathery head, but a bald head is easy to keep clean.

Turkey vultures don't pee on one another, but they do pee on themselves. And it's no accident.

On hot days, human bodies keeps cool by producing a steady supply of clear, salty **SWEAT**. As the sweat **EVAPORATES**, or turns into a gas and rises into the air, the heat on the skin goes along for the ride.

But a turkey vulture can't make sweat. So it stays cool by peeing on its legs. As the urine evaporates, body heat escapes through the scales on the bird's legs.

GRAY WOLVES

olves use urine to communicate. About once a week, a pack of wolves patrols the edges of its territory. The lead wolf, called the alpha male, pees every few hundred feet. The strong scent sends a message to other wolves: "Go away, or you'll be sorry."

If wolves didn't mark their territory with urine, other animals wouldn't know they weren't welcome. Scent marking is one way that wolves avoid fighting with one another.

34

A packrat loves to collect all kinds of things in its nest—from pinecones and earrings to bones and bottle caps.

A packrat can't see very well, so it leaves a trail of itty-bitty urine droplets everywhere it goes. After a day of feeding on twigs, seeds, and fruit, the little critter sniffs its way home.

A packrat also urinates all over its huge nest to help locate it.

PACKRATS

HAGFISH

Hagfish have lived on Earth for at least 550 million years. That means they were swimming through the seas for 300 million years before the first dinosaurs appeared.

kay, okay, enough about pee. It's slime time. The icky, sticky slime we call snot is just one kind of **MUCUS**. Human bodies are full of the gooey stuff. It oozes down our throats, churns inside our stomachs, and even drips into our lungs.

Lots of other animals make mucus, too, and you wouldn't believe how they use it. Take the hagfish, for example. It uses slimy mucus to give enemies the slip.

When a bigger fish attacks, mucus pours out of a hagfish's body. The sticky goo traps the predator and clogs its **GILLS**. While the unhappy hunter struggles to escape, the hagfish swims to safety.

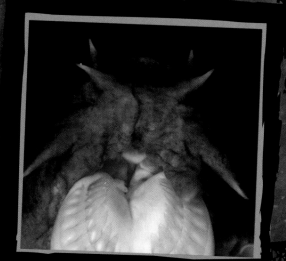

he tropical rain forest is a dangerous place, especially if you're small and tasty. So staying safe is a full-time job for a red-eyed tree frog. During the day, this leggy leaper spends most of its time clinging to the undersides of leaves. How does it get a grip? With the super-sticky mucus on the bottom of its toes.

When the little frog gets settled, it closes its bright red eyes. And it tucks its large orange feet under its body. Its light green body looks just like a leaf. What a great way to hide from enemies!

RED-EYED TREE FROGS

Red-eyed tree frogs live their whole lives high above the ground. At night, they feed on crickets, moths, flies, and other insects.

GARDEN SNAILS

Not many animals leave behind gooey trails wherever they go. But snails do.

Slimy mucus oozes out of a garden snail's muscular foot, smoothing its path across uneven ground. It also prevents a snail's soft, squishy body from drying out.

On damp days, a garden snail's slime pulls moisture out of the air. On dry days, it draws water out of the soil.

A banana slug's slimy mucus comes in handy. Besides helping the slug move, take in moisture, and avoid enemies, it also contains chemicals that attract other slugs at mating time.

peaking of slugs, a banana slug is bright and slimy. Bright colors tell other animals, "Don't eat me, or you'll be sorry."

Most predators won't try to eat a banana slug. But if they do, they'll really regret it. The slug's mucus makes an attacker's mouth go NUMB.

BANANA SLUGS

LATIA LIMPETS

During the day, Latia limpets creep along rocky streambeds and feed on tiny creatures.

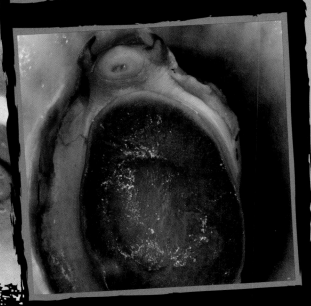

A limpet is a small snail with a dome-shaped shell. They live in oceans and in freshwater, too.

Latia limpets make their home on the rocky bottoms of New Zealand's small streams. To stay safe at night, they make glow-in-the-dark mucus.

When a hungry fish tries to pry a limpet off a rock, the snail releases a gob of glowing slime. As the greenish-yellow goo flows downstream, the attacker chases the moving light. Bye-bye, predator.

Everyone knows that fish are pretty slimy.

A fish has good reason to make all that gooey gunk. Two reasons, actually. It protects a fish's skin from harmful bacteria, and it also makes a fish's scales more flexible.

Some parrotfish have a third reason for making mucus. It helps them get a good night's sleep.

Every evening, the parrotfish wrap themselves up in a slimy cocoon. All night long, the tent of mucus keeps out the tiny blood-sucking creatures swimming nearby.

The slimy sacks really work. Parrotfish without a cocoon are 80 percent more likely to be attacked than fish shrouded in slime.

PARROTFISH

During the day, parrotfish chew chunks of coral to get at the tasty algae inside. Bones in their throat grind coral into sand. Believe it or not, we have parrotfish and other coral-crunching creatures to thank for many of the world's sandy beaches.

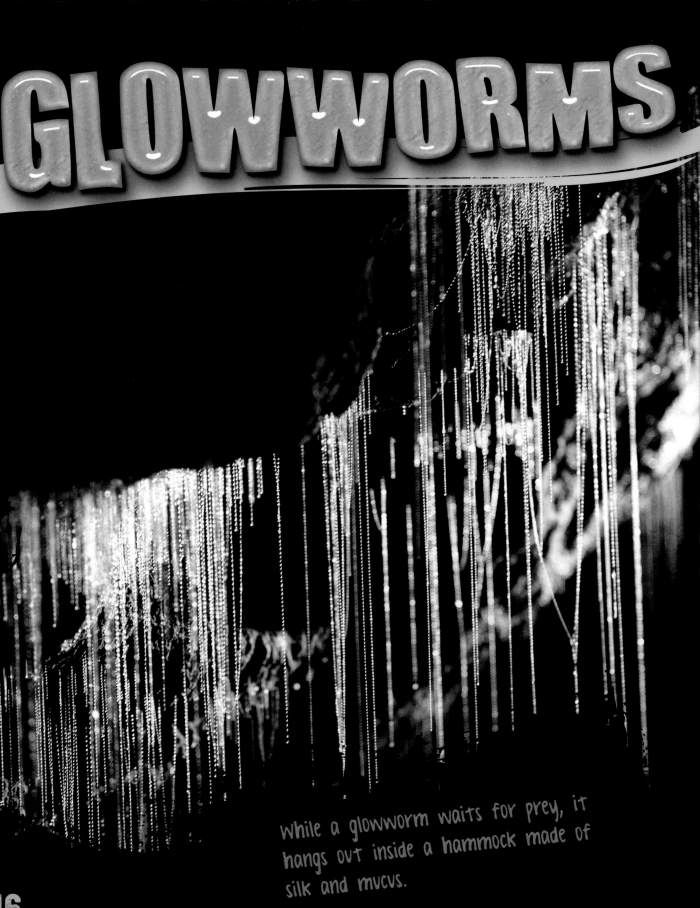

GLOWWORMS

While a glowworm waits for prey, it hangs out inside a hammock made of silk and mucus.

A glowworm's name is half right—and half wrong. Its bright back end really does light up the cave where it lives. But the little critter isn't a worm. It's a **LARVA**—a young insect. When a glowworm grows up, it becomes a fly.

A glowworm uses its blue-green tail light to catch **PREY**. First it builds a network of silk threads that hang down from the ceiling of its cave. Each thread is covered with drops of sticky mucus.

The larva's light makes the mucus glow. And that attracts insects. When a victim gets stuck in a thread, the glowworm reels it in, sucks out the juices, and spits out the rest.

When a hungry panther chameleon spots an insect, it doesn't waste any time. Faster than you can blink, its long tongue shoots out, catches the prey, and snaps back into its mouth. The lizard almost never misses a meal.

What's the secret to the chameleon's success? Actually, there are two: strong muscles and sticky mucus.

Powerful muscles on each side of the lizard's tongue tug on the tip, forming a pouch that acts like a suction cup. The instant that super sticky mucus nabs an unsuspecting insect, the tongue's suction power hurls the prey into the chameleon's mouth. The victim doesn't stand a chance!

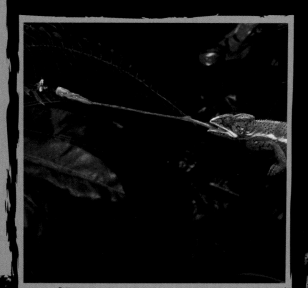

PANTHER CHAMELEONS

Panther chameleons live in the forests of Madagascar, a large island off the coast of Africa. Most of the time, their bodies are green. But they can turn orange, blue, or brown, depending on the temperature and their mood.

EARTHWORMS

An earthworm's body is mostly **PROTEIN,** so the little wrigglers make a very healthy snack. Maybe that's why some people in Australia, New Zealand, and China like to eat them.

An earthworm may have five hearts, but it doesn't have any lungs. And it doesn't have gills, either. So how does this creepy crawly critter get the **OXYGEN** it needs to survive? Through its skin.

But that can't happen without mucus. Once oxygen mixes with the icky goo covering an earthworm's body, it passes through the skin and into the blood vessels. Then blood delivers oxygen to all the earthworm's cells.

Mucus also traps moisture inside an earthworm's body. And it helps the little wriggler burrow through soil. Thank goodness for slime!

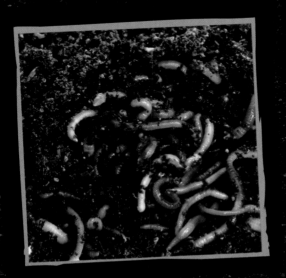

Lucky for frogs, it isn't very easy to catch them. That's because most frogs have slimy skin. Thick, gooey mucus keeps a frog's skin moist, so it can take in oxygen from the air.

A strawberry poison dart frog's slime is extra sticky. And it's a good thing, too.

Most frogs lay their eggs in the water. Their tadpoles start swimming the moment they hatch.

But strawberry poison dart frogs live in the treetops of tropical rain forests. They lay their eggs on leaves. When the tadpoles hatch, they climb onto their mom's back. Gummy goo stops the little ones from slipping and sliding.

STRAWBERRY POISON DART FROGS

Strawberry poison dart tadpoles grow up in pools that form among the leaves and flowers of plants that grow in rain forest canopies.

HOUSE CATS

As far as humans are concerned, licking yourself is considered bad manners.

But what seems wrong to us is perfectly normal for lots of other animals. Cats spend at least two hours a day slathering themselves with spit and then licking it off. It's their way of staying neat and tidy.

A cat's rough tongue is like a comb. It's perfect for picking up dirt, dust, and loose pieces of hair.

Some scientists are searching for ways to use mouse spit to heal human wounds faster.

ike cats, mice groom themselves when they want to clean up. But they also use spit to help heal wounds. When a mouse gets a cut, it spreads SALIVA on the injury. A protein in the spit attacks harmful bacteria before they can infect the injured area.

HOUSE MICE

YELLOW-BELLIED SAPSUCKERS

Yellow-bellied sapsuckers drill into all kinds of trees, but their favorite sap comes from birches and aspens. As these birds lap up sap, they also gobble up insects stuck in the sweet liquid.

A yellow-bellied sapsucker is a bird that makes sounds like a cat. And that's not the only strange thing about this little woodpecker.

Most woodpeckers drill holes in trees and use their long tongues to pry out insects. But not sapsuckers. They'd much rather dine on the tree's sugary sap.

When a sapsucker is hungry, it hammers through a tree's bark and starts to slurp. A chemical in sapsucker saliva keeps the tree's juices flowing. That means the bird can keep on sucking until it's had its fill.

ost people swallow about two thousand times a day. And each time, a flood of saliva washes down the throat.

How does the body keep up? Every day, it makes more than enough saliva to fill three pint-size milk cartons.

Sounds like whole a lot of spit, right? It's nothing compared to a cow's daily supply. Cattle—cows and bulls—make nearly a hundred times more spit every single day.

Why do cattle need so much saliva? Because they eat dry plants, like grass and hay. Their wet, slimy spit helps the food slide down their throats.

CATTLE

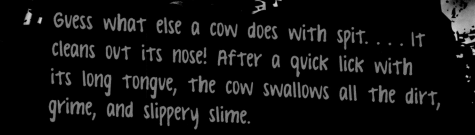

Guess what else a cow does with spit. . . . It cleans out its nose! After a quick lick with its long tongue, the cow swallows all the dirt, grime, and slippery slime.

GIRAFFES

A full-grown giraffe can be up to 19 feet tall and weigh as much as 2,800 pounds. A giraffe eats about 140 pounds of acacia per day.

Giraffes are the tallest animals on Earth. They tower high above the African plains they call home.

Using their long tongues, giraffes can easily grab leaves and twigs that other animals can't reach. That's the good news. But there's bad news, too. A giraffe's favorite food is the acacia tree. And sharp, spiky thorns line its branches!

Luckily, there's a solution. A giraffe makes lots of thick, gooey saliva. The spit coats the thorns and protects the inside of the animal's mouth.

Each spring, a queen bald-faced hornet begins building a new home. She chews up wood fibers and slathers them with spit. Then she spreads the pulpy mash with her legs and mouthparts. When the mixture dries, it forms the gray paper walls of her nest.

As the colony grows, the hornets expand their home, layer by layer. By the end of summer, a nest can be as big as a basketball and have paper walls more than two inches thick!

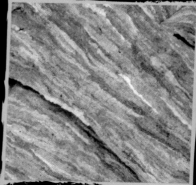

How many hornets can live inside a large nest? As many as seven hundred!

BALD-FACED HORNETS

Inside the nest, the bald-faced hornet queen lays eggs all summer long. Workers feed and care for the larvae and watch over the **PUPAE.**

SPITTLEBUGS

As a spittlebug sucks on plant juices it grows quickly. After shedding its skin five times, it becomes an adult insect called a froghopper.

What's lurking inside the bubbly white froth in this picture? A spittlebug. The foamy home is the perfect place to hide from enemies. And the sudsy slather keeps the young insect's body warm at night and moist during the day.

Spittle looks like saliva, but it's not. It's made of plant juices. After the spittlebug sucks the liquid up, it mixes with air and other materials from glands inside its body. They form a white goo that shoots out the insect's back end. Then the youngster uses its back legs to whip the gooey spittle into a mass of bubbly foam.

A short-tailed shrew sure looks cute and cuddly. But watch out for this little critter! It has one heck of a bite.

When a short-tailed shrew spots a wriggling earthworm or a slimy slug, it pounces on the prey. As it sinks its teeth into the helpless victim, poisonous saliva PARALYZES the animal's entire body.

If the shrew is hungry, it eats the food right away. But if not, it can also save the meal for later. The paralyzed animal won't be able to move a muscle for about two weeks.

SHORT-TAILED SHREWS

A short-tailed shrew eats up to three times its body weight in food each day. That would be like a 70-pound kid eating 840 hamburgers every single day.

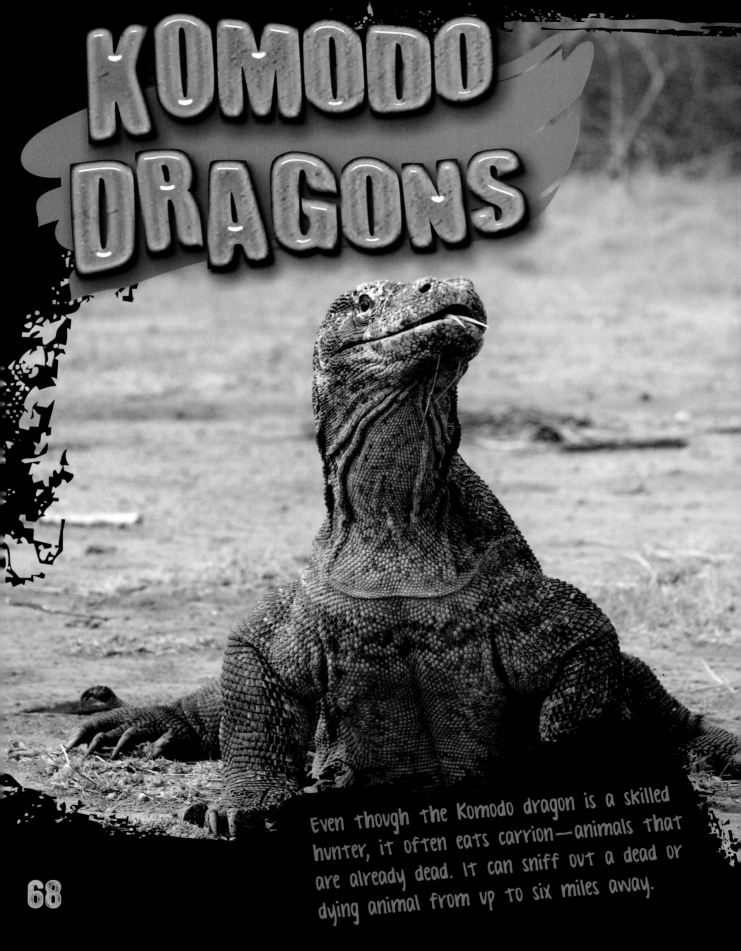

KOMODO DRAGONS

Even though the Komodo dragon is a skilled hunter, it often eats carrion—animals that are already dead. It can sniff out a dead or dying animal from up to six miles away.

The Komodo dragon is the largest lizard alive today. It can grow to nearly 10 feet long and weigh as much as 150 pounds! But size isn't the only thing that makes this monstrous reptile a fearsome predator.

When a Komodo dragon spots a deer, goat, or wild boar, it lunges forward and grabs the prey by the throat. Sure, the lizard has sharp teeth. But its spit is just as deadly. It's swarming with harmful bacteria that infect the victim's wounds.

Sometimes a Komodo dragon's prey manages to escape. But that's no problem. The patient predator just follows the injured animal until it dies.

Fish. Frogs. Snails. Snakes. They're no match for a giant water bug. Not even close.

When a giant water bug rests on the bottom of a pond, it looks just like a dead leaf. Larger animals don't even notice the hungry hunter—until it's too late.

A water bug seizes prey with its powerful front legs. Then it thrusts its beak deep inside the victim. Powerful chemicals in the bug's saliva go to work right away. They digest the helpless animal's body from the inside out. Then the water bug sucks out the juices.

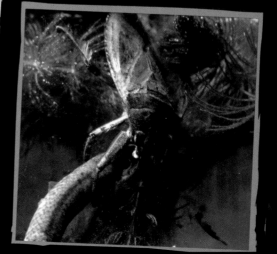

GIANT WATER BUGS

Believe it or not, a giant water bug breathes through its behind. See those two little tubes on its back end? When the insect needs oxygen, it lifts them above the water's surface and takes in air.

PIGS

People have been raising pigs for meat for at least seven thousand years. A female pig gives birth once or twice a year and can have more than a dozen piglets at a time.

Pigs are known for being dirty and smelly and not particularly attractive. Well, except to other pigs. And that's because they have irresistible spit.

At mating time, a male pig starts cranking out saliva full of a chemical that drives the girls crazy. When a female pig sniffs a whiff of that sweet saliva scent, she knows she's found the perfect male.

Believe it or not, perfume companies have tried adding the charming chemicals in pig spit to their products. But they don't seem to have the same effect on human females.

O n a really hot day, ten liters' worth of sweat can trickle out of your sweat glands. As all that sweat evaporates, it removes the heat from your skin.

A dog can't sweat through its thick fur, so it cools off by panting. When the spit in a dog's mouth heats up, it evaporates—just like sweat.

As the dog's tongue cools down, so does the blood inside it. Then the dog's hardworking heart pumps the cooled blood to the rest of its body. Slowly but surely, the dog's whole body cools off.

DOGS

While resting, a dog breathes about ten to thirty times a minute. But when a dog is panting to cool off, its respiration rate may soar as high as four hundred breaths per minute.

FENNEC FOXES

A fennec fox's sandy fur reflects heat from the sun. It also blends in perfectly with the animal's desert surroundings. Extra fur on the bottoms of the fox's feet helps it move quickly across loose sand.

he fennec fox is the smallest member of the fox family, but it has the biggest ears. And it's a good thing, too.

Big ears help the little hunter survive in the sizzling-hot Sahara desert. Sure, they're perfect for hearing tasty insects and lizards as they scurry across the sand. But those oversize ears do much more than that. They also help the fox cool off.

Instead of sweating or panting, a fennec fox loses body heat through the thin skin on its enormous ears. And that cools the blood inside. As that blood travels through the fox's **CIRCULATORY SYSTEM**, its entire body cools down.

Vampire bats get their name from feasting on blood. Why blood? Because it's full of nutrients. Vampire bats feed on all kinds of warm-blooded animals—birds, cows, pigs, goats, and deer. Special sensors on a bat's face can target a victim by detecting its body heat. The sensors also help the bat bite its prey in places where blood flows just below the skin.

Vampire bats gulp down 70 to 80 percent of their body weight each night. As soon as the little bloodsuckers finish a meal, they urinate. They have to get rid of the water weight before they can fly.

VAMPIRE BATS

If a vampire bat is sick, other bats will feed it. They **REGURGITATE** blood they have recently drank so the sick bat can lap it up.

VAMPIRE FINCHES

Vampire bats aren't the only animals that feed on blood. The vampire finch usually eats seeds and insects, but it can't resist a yummy blood meal. When it spots a blue-footed booby, it pecks at the larger bird's skin until blood starts to flow. Scientists aren't sure why the larger birds don't fight back.

Vampire finches live on the Galápagos Islands, a group of islands off the west coast of South America.

Madrilenial butterflies live in Spain. They often feed right along with flesh flies, vultures, and other scavengers.

Delicate and *graceful* are some of the words often used to describe butterflies.

But consider the madrilenial butterfly.

NECTAR isn't the only thing it sips with its strawlike PROBOSCIS. It also feeds on the blood of any dead animal it can find.

MADRILENIAL BUTTERFLIES

MOSQUITOES

What makes that annoying whine you hear when a mosquito flies by? Its wings. They beat up to six hundred times a second, propelling a mosquito through the air at a speed of two to three miles per hour.

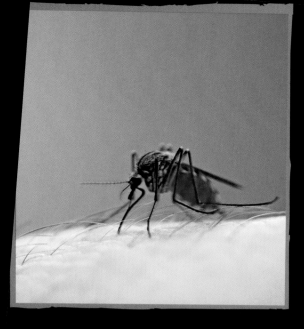

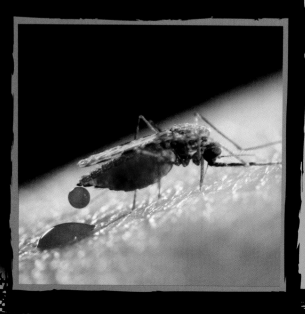

There are a whole bunch of little creepy crawlies that feast on blood. Fleas. Ticks. Bedbugs. Leeches. And of course, mosquitoes.

However, male mosquitoes never drink a single drop of blood. They feed on nectar their whole lives.

Females sip nectar, too—most of the time. So what's the reason for all those mosquito bites? Mothers. Mama mosquitoes need the iron and proteins in blood to make the yolk for their eggs. The yolk in each egg is a source of food for the developing larva.

GARDEN SPIDERS

ake a look at this giant garden spider. Don't worry. It doesn't drink blood from other animals. But it does use its own blood in a way that might surprise you. When a spider **MOLTS**, or sheds its skin, its heart pumps extra blood into the front of its body. The blood pushes on the old skin until it cracks open.

Did you know a spider's blood is blue, not red? That's because it contains different proteins than our blood.

Elephant seals are huge animals. They can weigh as much as 7,780 pounds.

Humans may be able to hold their breath for two minutes. But northern elephant seals can hold their breath for two hours!

How do they do it? Their blood can hold extra oxygen. Lots of it. They need all that air to dive down thousands of feet in search of tasty squid and fish.

ELEPHANT SEALS

A horned lizard might be small, but it sure knows how to survive. First, it scurries away from a predator and then suddenly stops. The lizard's sandy scales make it almost invisible in its desert surroundings.

If that doesn't work, the lizard hisses fiercely and puffs up its body to look as large as possible. It may also try to stab the attacker with its horns and spines.

If none of these strategies send the enemy running, the resourceful reptile tries one more trick. It startles the predator by squirting blood out of the corners of its eyes.

HORNED LIZARDS

To squirt blood, a horned lizard reduces the amount of blood flowing out of its head. As **BLOOD PRESSURE** builds up, small blood vessels around its eyelids burst open, spurting blood up to three feet.

CAMELS

The color of a camel's puke depends on what it's been eating. If a camel dines on grass, its vomit will be green.

O f course, humans don't purposely vomit on one another—even if they're in a fight! But believe it or not, a camel would—without giving it a second thought.

When a camel gets mad, it regurgitates its last meal. Then it uses its tongue and limp, droopy lips to fling the chunky goo at other animals.

It turns out llamas and alpacas do the same thing.

GRASSHOPPERS

It's not such a good idea to pick up a grasshopper. The startled insect will leave behind a wet, stinky brown puddle. You might think it's spit or maybe pee. Actually, it's a heap of partially digested food. That's right—puke.

It's hard to hold on to a grasshopper for long. These leggy leapers can jump up to twenty times their body length.

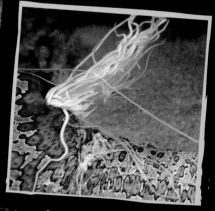

Sea cucumbers hang out on shallow seafloors all over the world. They are closely related to sea stars, sea urchins, and sand dollars.

Some sea cucumbers use a similar trick to startle their enemies. When a predator attacks, the pickle-like ocean animal pukes up its INTESTINES. This is enough to make most predators lose their appetite.

SEA CUCUMBERS

FROGS

Frogs have managed to survive on Earth for two hundred million years. Humans have only been around for about two million years.

When humans eat food their bodies don't like, they throw up.

Believe it or not, a frog can take things a step further. It doesn't just lose its last meal. It ejects its entire stomach, turning the organ inside out.

And that's not all. Once the frog's stomach pops outside its body, the little amphibian uses its front legs to scrape out all the partially digested food. Then the frog swallows, pulling its empty stomach back into its body.

Never seen a giant petrel? That's no surprise. They live where most people don't—along the coasts of Antarctica and other islands in the Southern Ocean.

These seabirds soar through the sky in search of squid and fish. And if they don't get their fill, they hunt for carcasses along the shore. Petrels think dead seals, penguins, and whales are tasty treats.

After a big meal, giant petrels are too heavy to fly. So they nap on the beach while their food digests.

What happens if a predator tries to attack? No problem. The birds vomit until they're light enough to take flight.

GIANT PETRELS

With wings that span up to six feet, giant petrels are skilled, graceful fliers. They can cruise through the air for hours at a time.

A housefly will eat almost anything. If the food is liquid, the fly just sucks it up. But if it's solid, things get a bit more complicated. After all, a fly doesn't have teeth.

The fly ejects a mix of saliva and digestive juices from its stomach. The vomit breaks down food from the outside in. Then the fly mops up the meal with its spongelike mouthparts.

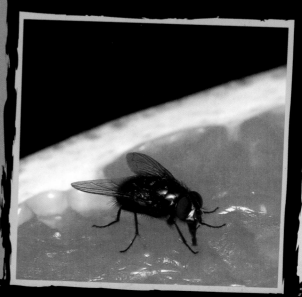

HOUSEFLIES

Houseflies don't just eat the food they land on. They also lay their eggs in it. That's one more reason to swat the little pests away from your supper.

JACKALS

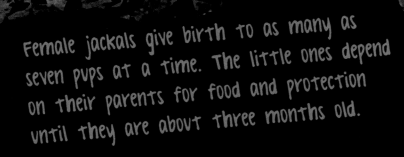

Female jackals give birth to as many as seven pups at a time. The little ones depend on their parents for food and protection until they are about three months old.

What do jackals have in common with houseflies? They aren't picky eaters. As part of nature's cleanup crew, the sneaky scavengers don't let a thing go to waste.

Jackals scarf down whatever meat lions and leopards leave behind—even if it's swarming with maggots and has been rotting for days.

When a mama jackal has had her fill, she heads back to her den and pukes the partially digested mush up for her pups.

What happens if the pups' eyes are bigger than their stomachs? No worries. Their mother re-eats the leftovers.

ackals aren't the only animals that feed their youngsters puke. Lots of birds do it, including penguins.

When a penguin chick hatches, its body is covered with soft, warm down feathers. Down is great for protecting a chick from wind and cold, but it isn't waterproof. And that's a problem, because a penguin's food comes from the sea.

So until a chick's adult feathers grow in, it dines on partially digested fish and squid provided by its parents. A few hours after eating, the adult regurgitates part of its meal into its beak. Then it feeds the mushy mash into the youngster's mouth.

PENGUINS

Feeding a chick is a big job, so most female penguins lay just one egg at a time.

OWLS

Owl pellets are often made up of bones, fur, feathers, and other materials that cannot be digested.

Can you imagine vomiting every day? Well that's what owls do.

An owl doesn't have teeth, so it swallows prey whole. But the bird's body can't break down bones or fur or feathers. So about twenty hours after eating, an owl regurgitates a slimy pellet of hard, indigestible materials.

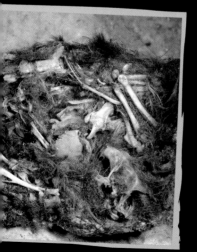

WHITE-TAILED DEER

Because it takes so much work to digest food, deer spend lots of time eating. An average-size deer chows down about eight pounds of food a day—that's about four times more than an average-size person eats.

Everything a white-tailed deer eats comes back up two, three, maybe even four times. And each time, the deer chews the cud (partially digested food) a little bit more. With every re-swallowing, bacteria inside the animal's **DIGESTIVE SYSTEM** get another chance to feast on the cud and help break down the tough plant materials.

Deer are not the world's only cud chewers. Cattle, goats, sheep, giraffes, camels, buffalo, llamas, wildebeest, antelope, and more than one hundred other large plant-eating mammals all regurgitate their cud until the nutrients are ready to enter their blood and travel to their cells.

Everyone knows bees make sweet, syrupy honey, but the process is grosser than expected.

First, a field bee sucks up nectar from dozens of flowers. Back at the hive, she vomits the nectar and a house bee swallows it.

Little by little, the house bee regurgitates the sugary puke and rolls it around in her mouth. As the mixture warms up and mixes with bee spit, it thickens into honey.

So the next time you have some honey, you'll know exactly what you're eating!

HONEYBEES

Using her long, strawlike proboscis, the house bee (left) is sucking nectar out of a field bee's mouth. When she is done, the field bee will head back out to collect more nectar.

WORDS TO KNOW

BACTERIA—Tiny, one-celled living things that reproduce by dividing. Some bacteria help your body function. Others can make you sick.

BLADDER—The body organ that holds urine before it is released from the body.

BLOOD PRESSURE—The pressure of the blood in the circulatory system. It is closely related to the force and rate of the heartbeat.

CECOTROPES—Soft, shiny pellets full of partially digested food that are eaten by the animal that produces them so the contents can be more fully digested.

CIRCULATORY SYSTEM—The parts of the body that transport blood throughout the body.

DIGEST—To break down food.

DIGESTIVE SYSTEM—The parts of the body involved in breaking down food and absorbing nutrients.

DUNG—Poop.

DWELLING—Home; the place where an animal lives.

EVAPORATE—To change from a liquid to a gas.

FERTILIZE—In farming, to add nutrients that encourage growth.

FUNGUS (PL. FUNGI)—A one-celled or multicelled living thing. Its body is made of thin threads that absorb nutrients.

GILLS—Body organs that fish and many other animals that live in water use to take in oxygen.

INTESTINE—The part of the digestive system that breaks down food particles and allows nutrients to pass into the blood. It's often divided into the small intestine and large intestine.

LARVA (PL. LARVAE)—The second stage in the life of some insects. The term is also used to describe young amphibians and some other kinds of animals.

MAMMAL—A warm-blooded animal that has a backbone and feeds mother's milk to its young. Almost all mammals have some hair or fur.

MARSUPIAL—A kind of mammal that gives birth to very small babies and protects them inside a stomach pouch for several months.

MOLT—To shed an old outer covering that is worn out or too small.

MUCUS—A slimy mixture that coats many surfaces inside the body. In the respiratory system it stops germs, dirt, pollen, and other foreign particles from reaching the lungs.

NECTAR—A sugary liquid that many flowers produce. It attracts insects that spread the plant's pollen.

NUMB—Unable to move or act.

NUTRIENT—A substance that keeps the body healthy. It comes from food.

OXYGEN—An invisible gas that animals need to live.

PARALYZE—To make unable to move or act.

PREDATOR—An animal that hunts and kills other animals for food.

PREY—An animal that is hunted by a predator.

PROBOSCIS—A long, straw-like body part that some insects, including bees and butterflies, use to suck nectar.

PROTEIN—A molecule that speeds up chemical reactions, repairs damaged cells, and builds new bones, teeth, hair, muscles, and skin.

PUPA (PL. PUPAE)—The third stage in the life of some insects.

REGURGITATE—To vomit. *Puke*, *barf*, and *upchuck* are also words that can mean "vomit" or "to vomit."

SALIVA—A watery liquid that contains gases, salts, mucus, and proteins that break down food and destroy bacteria living in your mouth. It is also called spit.

SWEAT—A salty liquid that is released from sweat glands in the skin. It helps people and some other animals cool off.

Amazing Animals of the World. New York, NY: Scholastic Library, 2006.*

Attenborough, David. *The Life of Birds.* Princeton, NJ: Princeton University Press, 1998.

Carwardine, Mark and Rosamund Kidman Cox. *Extreme Nature.* New York, NY: Harper, 2005.

Eisner, Thomas. *For Love of Insects.* Cambridge, MA: Harvard University Press, 2005.

Goodman, Susan E. *The Truth About Poop.* New York, NY: Viking, 2004.*

Goodman, Susan E. *Gee Whiz! It's All About Pee.* New York, NY: Viking, 2006.*

Stewart, Melissa. *It's Spit-acular!: The Secrets of Saliva.* Tarrytown, NY: Benchmark Books, 2009.

Tabak, Lawrence A. and Robert Kuska. "Mouth to Mouth." *Natural History.* November 2004.

Trudee, Romanek. *Squirt!: The Most Interesting Book You'll Ever Read About Blood.* Toronto, Ontario, Canada: Kids Can Press, 2006.*

Waldbauer, Gilbert. *A Walk Around the Pond: Insects in and over the Water.* Cambridge, MA: Harvard University Press, 2006.

*Recommended for curious kids.